UNIVERSITY OF MINNESOTA

⌁ *Vladimir Nabokov*

BY JULIAN MOYNAHAN

UNIVERSITY OF MINNESOTA PRESS • MINNEAPOLIS

Printed in the United States of America at
the North Central Publishing Company, St. Paul

Library of Congress Catalog Card Number: 71-633325
ISBN 0-8166-0600-5

Thanks are due to Professor Clarence Brown of the Princeton
Slavic Department for the gift of a proof copy of Karl Proffer's
Keys to Lolita and for sharing his learned views on Nabokov.

Dates in the text placed in parentheses after titles are those of
first publication in the language in which the work
was originally composed.

PUBLISHED IN GREAT BRITAIN, INDIA, AND PAKISTAN BY THE OXFORD
UNIVERSITY PRESS, LONDON, BOMBAY, AND KARACHI, AND IN CANADA
BY THE COPP CLARK PUBLISHING CO. LIMITED, TORONTO

For man has closed himself up, till he sees all things thro' narrow chinks of his cavern.

— William Blake

JULIAN MOYNAHAN teaches English at Rutgers University and is the author of the novels *Sisters and Brothers* and *Pairing Off* as well as a critical study of D. H. Lawrence entitled *The Deed of Life.*

⌐ *Vladimir Nabokov*

Since Proust we have accepted the view that memory is an art, maybe the sole art to have survived God's death, and that nostalgia may encapsulate a metaphysic. Until V. V. Nabokov came to America in 1940 we Americans had no great modern artist in nostalgia of our own, although F. Scott Fitzgerald strikes the authentic note when he imagines Nick Carraway observing Gatsby waiting for the green light in the closing paragraphs of *The Great Gatsby*. Gatsby mistakes the past for the future — the characteristic error of nostalgists — when he anticipates a reunion with Daisy, that shopworn Louisville Lolita, which "was already behind him, somewhere back in that vast obscurity beyond the city, where the dark fields of the republic rolled on under the night." And Fitzgerald's power of evocation in this instance arises from the fact, tragic for his entire career, that he too is a nostalgist, "borne back ceaselessly into the past," victim of a disposition and attitude he rarely was able to command for the servicing of his art.

"Nostalgist" is a graceless term. In *Pale Fire* Nabokov coins the expression "preterist: one who collects cold nests" for the artist who commands the past qua past, never confusing it with present and future although his created characters may do so, and drawing from this beguiling imaginative realm rich material for an art of memory which illuminates the whole range of time through which the artist has lived. Considering William Faulkner's obsession with lapsed time in his Yoknapatawpha County sequence we might think that he before Nabokov is the great American artist of preterism. Yet in Faulkner time is spatialized, into an echoing corridor where characters like Quentin Compson and Rosa Coldfield run furiously, doing battle with ghosts from Civil War times and earlier; or it is frozen into a hallucinatory instant when ghostly men-at-arms relive at close of day their moment of glorious risk under the rapt eye of a defeated eccentric like the Reverend Gail Hightower.

Preterist art, by contrast, works in a cooler, more classical fashion. Both Proust and Nabokov establish clear boundaries between past and present, provide elaborate and meticulously drafted maps for their realms of recollection, and carefully choose the grounds, or privileged moments, at which past and present will be allowed, briefly and dangerously, to meet and commingle. The goal of these artists is something more important than self-discovery or the discovery of cultural and regional identity. It is the discovery and definition of human consciousness, conceived as the master key to the riddle of reality, conceived also as providing limited, transitory glimpses of the realm of essence.

Neither Proust nor Nabokov permits this essentially metaphysical quest to sterilize his fictional art. Both remain great tragicomic novelists in close touch with the actualities of man in contemporary society and with central issues of modern history. Thirst for the eternal never alienates their loyalty to the human condition although it may constitute the deepest source of their great originality and power as stylists and fabulists. In the following pages I shall try to indicate the range, charm, and contemporary relevance of Nabokov's prose artistry without, I hope, ever quite losing sight of his cunning, wholly devoted pursuit of certain overwhelming questions which the publicists of the death of God once thought, mistakenly, to have put to death as well.

Nabokov was born in 1899 into a rich, accomplished, and socially enlightened St. Petersburg family which had given admirals, scholars, and statesmen to the Russian nation over many generations. He enjoyed a privileged and secure boyhood, dividing his time between the beautiful Nabokov country estate called Vyra and a town house ample and elegant enough to accommodate under the Soviets a foreign diplomatic mission and later a school of architecture. He attended an excellent and progressive school in the city and spent his holidays at the country estate, where he became an expert tennis player and amateur lepidopterist, and on the French Riviera, to which the Nabokovs were accustomed to travel annually by train to enjoy sea bathing and the sedate life in luxurious hotels led by the high European bourgeoisie of that vanished time.

This Edenic phase was abruptly terminated when Vladimir's father, who had been a leading member of the Russian Constituent Assembly, took his family south to Yalta to avoid the Red armies of the Bolshevik Revolution and, upon the collapse of White military resistance in the Crimea, fled with them into exile in Western Europe.

Between 1919 and 1922 Vladimir, who had learned English thoroughly from governesses and tutors while a small child, studied modern languages and literature at Trinity College, Cambridge. After graduating with first-class honors he rejoined his family in Berlin and set about launching a career as an émigré poet, critic, and novelist. In 1922 his beloved and admired father fell victim to a pair of Russian right-monarchist gunmen while chairing a political meeting and Vladimir, the oldest son, became head of a family for which the condition of exile from its native country was destined to be permanent.

Throughout the 1920's and 1930's, writing in Russian under the pen name V. Sirin and residing first in Berlin and then in Paris, Nabokov produced a brilliant series of poems, stories, and novels which established him as unquestionably the most gifted Russian writer-in-exile of his generation. At the same time, his attitude toward the endless political intrigues, fantasies of imminent Romanov restoration, religious manias, and literary cabals of the Rus-

7

sian émigré circles centering on Berlin, Prague, and Paris remained detached, ironic, and independent. He suffered with his fellow Russians the inconvenience and indignity of the Nansen passport, issued by the League of Nations to stateless persons, and financial problems at times forced him into such temporary extraliterary expedients as coaching tennis, teaching language, and composing chess problems for magazines. But there was no extended period during the difficult first two decades of his career when he was deflected from his main task — the creation of a major literary oeuvre in Russian, culminating in *Dar* or *The Gift* (1938), a masterpiece of wit, poetic fantasy, and stylistic games which remains, in my opinion, one of his three finest novels as well as one of the great books of twentieth-century literature in any language.

In 1940 when Nabokov departed for America, accompanied by his wife Véra and young son Dmitri, a new twenty-year phase of his career opened. Begun in the distress and obscurity of a second exile during wartime, it was to turn, but not fully until after 1955 and the publication of *Lolita*, into an extraordinary, and perhaps peculiarly American, success story. As early as 1939, while still in France, he had begun to write in English, no doubt in wary anticipation of an impending move to England or America as Hitler's troops were massing to overrun Western Europe as far as the Atlantic. He settled first in the Boston area, taught Russian literature at Wellesley while simultaneously conducting scientific research in lepidopterology at the Harvard Entomological Museum, and brought out his first full-length literary work in English, the beguiling and melancholy *The Real Life of Sebastian Knight*, in 1941.

Over approximately the next decade and a half there occurred the amazing transformation of this middle-aged, twice-exiled European artist, scientist, and scholar into the great American author whom the world acknowledges today. His stories and verses and the chapters of his memoir about his Russian and European years appearing in the *New Yorker* during the late 1940's and early 1950's, which showed a constantly expanding command of English written style and its American vernacular adjuncts, established him with an American audience. At Cornell, where he taught Russian literature for some ten years after leaving Boston, he was able to pursue the nostalgic yet profound studies in Pushkin which culminated in his monumental four-volume translation of *Eugene Onegin* with commentaries (1964). Cornell also exposed him to the pleasures, pangs, pomps, and bizarreries of American academic life, an experience he would put richly to use in writing the comic and touching prose sketches that make up *Pnin* (1957) and the third of his three greatest books, *Pale Fire* (1962). Even the long American academic vacations made a signal contribution, for it was during summers away from Cornell, while traveling extensively through North America on butterfly-hunting expeditions, that he became familiar with the ambiance of highways and byways, the subculture of motels, filling stations, frazzled eateries, and bypassed, desperate resorts which contribute so sinister and pitiful a flavor to the imaginative environment of *Lolita*.

Publication of *Lolita*, the second of his triumvirate of masterpieces, in 1955, marks the full emergence of the butterfly from the chrysalis, the point at which Nabokov was able to come at long last into full control of his artistic destiny. The book's financial success permitted him to resign his Cornell post, and a much-enhanced interest in all aspects of Nabokov's work throughout the English-speaking world has led over the past decade to the publication in excellent English translations (most of them by his son Dmitri) of nearly all the novels and novellas he had brought out in Russian during the twenties and thirties. This important project, which is still under way, has won a magical second life for the work of Nabokov's pre-American career while simplifying the task of evaluating his total achievement in fiction and confirming his position in the forefront of modern writers.

Since 1960 Nabokov has lived abroad once again, in Montreux, Switzerland. He remains an American citizen, revisits the United States frequently, and continues to affirm an affectionate attachment to this country in recent published interviews. Although he turned seventy in 1969 and was honored by a festschrift to which a wide international array of critics, scholars, and creative writers contributed, he is still in full career as a writer himself. In 1967 he brought out his own Russian translation of *Lolita* and 1969 saw publication of *Ada; or Ardor*, a quarter-million-word "family chronicle" novel in English, conceived in a rather baroque stylistic vein and containing some spectacular erotic episodes along with an elaborate plot, a stunningly original setting, and a lengthy terminal essay on the nature of time. Not now, and it is to be hoped, not for many years to come, can a critical commentator pretend to say the last word about this, as it were, amphibious Russian and American creative personality.

Speak, Memory (1951, revised edition 1966), called *Conclusive Evidence* in the British edition and *Drugiye Berega* (Other Shores) in a less well known and partly variant Russian version, is both an autobiography covering Nabokov's first forty-one years and a carefully shaped work of art devoted to the muse of memory, "Mnemosyne." For our purposes it provides a bridge between its author's lived experience and his re-creation of that experience in writing; and, not surprisingly, because it is a creative work of first rank, it reveals themes, conceptions, and images which one finds in various combinations and enlargements in his fiction proper.

It begins, rather like the famous first chapter of Dickens' *Great Expectations*, with an account of the infant child's awakening to consciousness. Awareness of self is born simultaneously with an awareness of an imprisonment in time, a time stranded between two eternities of darkness, all-past and all-future, a time defined as "walls . . . separating me and my bruised fists from the free world of timelessness," a prison that "is spherical and without exits." Rebellion against this tragic state of affairs is also born with consciousness of it and seeks in consciousness itself — in the heightening of consciousness we call imagination — a way out. There is no way out "short of suicide." This is surely one master idea in all of Nabokov's work. Yet through consciousness, through reflection on the riddling and cryptic appearances of the world, both outer and inner, in which the prisoner finds himself immured, he begins to discover or invent patterns, themes, repetitions, which hint at or gesture toward a possibility of transcendence into "the free world of timelessness" from which he has been banished through the catastrophic accident of biologic birth. And art, supremely, is the reflection of consciousness through which these discoveries become possible.

If the world is made of cryptic and riddling appearances, what can the prisoner discover, even through the agency of imagination, that amounts to more than deception piled on deception, *trompe l'oeil* painting on a prison wall? In chapter one of *Speak, Memory* Nabokov tells of General Kuropatkin, a visitor to the St. Petersburg house who amused the five-year-old Vladimir by arranging matches on the divan, first horizontally to form the sea in calm weather and then zigzag to form a stormy sea. The matches were scattered when the General, interrupted by an aide, rushed off to take command of — and to lose! — Russia's war in the Far East against Japan. Fifteen years later, when Nabokov's father was fleeing to southern Russia, he encountered on a bridge a gray-bearded peasant who asked him for a light. It was General Kuropatkin in disguise.

Here Nabokov remarks, "What pleases me is the evolution of the match theme," and we shall not take his point at all if we take the story altogether unseriously. The difference between the General, mocked by riddling destiny in the matter of matches, and Nabokov, reflecting upon a "repetitional theme," is considerable. Both the writer and the General are prisoners of contingency but the latter abides in dungeon darkness while the former has found a light by which he can see and reflect upon where and what he is. Thus, at the beginning of *Drugiye Berega*, Nabokov can speak of his autobiographical aim which is "to describe the past with utmost precision and to discover in it extraordinary outlines: namely, the development and repetition of hidden themes in the midst of one's overt destiny"; and, near the beginning of *Speak, Memory*, he can mention "the anonymous roller that pressed upon my life a certain intricate watermark whose unique design becomes visible when the lamp of art is made to shine through life's foolscap." The artist is at least free to spy out and to pursue, in the light of art, patterns removed from the domain of the absurd and meaningless by virtue of the mere fact that they *are*, visibly, of a certain shape and design: "the following of such thematic designs through one's life should be . . . the true purpose of autobiography."

Nevertheless, the basic theme is imprisonment, and Nabokov's novels are full of characters like Humbert Humbert whose frenzied pursuit of a certain "thematic design" called nymphets serves only to confirm his squalid, pitiful, and pathological enslavement. If liberation into timelessness is a real goal then all this activity of hunting down and following up, this spying and descrying in the light of consciousness and conscious art, falls far short of a real attained freedom. On Nabokov's own terms, is not the distinction between the artist-autobiographer and the unfortunate General simply the difference between a prisoner who takes exercise by creeping along the walls of his cell, holding aloft a guttering candle or feeble battery flashlight, and one who stays still in darkness waiting for death? They are both serving a life sentence and who therefore is to say that the less active one has made the worse adjustment?

This conclusion ignores a second great resource of the artist and autobiographer blessed with the power of imaginative reflection — his gift for making images. Toward the end of *Speak, Memory* Nabokov gaily describes the impact of the writings of the youthful and brilliant V. Sirin on Russian readers raised "on the sturdy straightforwardness of Russian realism." These readers, who were not in on the secret that Sirin and Nabokov are the same person, "were impressed by the mirror-like angles of his clear but weirdly misleading sentences and by the fact that the real life of his books flowed in his figures of speech, which one critic has compared to 'windows giving upon a contiguous world . . . a rolling corollary, the shadow of a train of thought.' "

The anonymous critic, who is certainly Nabokov himself in still another playful disguise, points up with the first of his comparisons the transcendent function of aesthetic images in Nabokov's work. Images are openings. Made out of words and from the materials of contingent experience, they paradoxically and magically create apertures in the walls of imprisoning time, transparencies which let in light from the free world of timelessness. Nabokov says of his own early works that the best "are those in which he condemns his people to the solitary confinement of their own souls." Actually, it is a cruelly true remark about all of his best works. But there is a way out, or at least a way of seeing out, for those who have sufficient imagination to fashion or discover an opening into timelessness. A number of Nabokov's "people," early and late, are driven to madness and death through their devotion to false images. Yet these failures, which must be seen finally as failures of imagination, of the image-making function in a generic sense, are never meant to suggest that the pursuit of transcendence through imagination should be abandoned as a hopeless project. If, for Nabokov, man is in prison, and if even the true images that he may descry or invent through artful intensities of consciousness tend, as they do in Yeats's great meditation on image making, "Among School Children," to break the heart by mocking man's contingency, the images still remain the only clue to the only thing worth attending to — the nature of the reality that lies outside the prison wall. The search for windows remains fundamental to Nabokov's powerfully imagistic art: there are really no alternatives, except a collapse of consciousness or the physical act of suicide.

Speak, Memory itself sumptuously and cunningly triumphs over lapsed time and uses the master image of apertures to do so. At the beginning the author sees "the awakening of consciousness as a series of spaced flashes, with the intervals between them gradually diminishing until bright blocks of perception are formed, affording memory a slippery hold." By the third chapter these perceptual blocks have stopped dancing and the author can refer, more straightforwardly, to "the act of vividly recalling a patch of the past." By now the method of the book, which is to deal in separate chapters with a single block, patch, image, or frame of recalled experience, has become clear. But method and content fuse as he recalls certain crucial early experiences and scenes involving windows and introduces the bright patches constituted by stained glass and butterfly specimens into the account of his growing up on the family estate. The train windows of the St. Petersburg to Paris Express dominate in the seventh chapter, and the vertiginous experience of glimpsing bright flashes of landscape outside the rushing train reinforces the original account of infant consciousness as a series of spaced flashes. Nabokov begins chapter eight by remarking casually that he is going to show a few "slides" and within the chapter manages to put together the account of an actual Magic-Lantern Projection evening arranged by his tutor with a recollection of his discovery of the beauty of glass slides seen in work with the microscope. The latter were "translucent miniatures, pocket wonderlands, neat little worlds of hushed luminous hues" where, while

---

contemplating this particular form of bright patch, he found a "delicate meeting place between imagination and knowledge."

In the context of memory this delicate meeting place is what the whole book is exploring; and the possibility of such exploration depends on the imagery of bright patches framed in an aperture. Even the boldly colored comic strips brought to him from America by his uncle — characteristically he is more interested in the pointillist technique of their reproduction than in the story they tell — become part of the pattern; as does "one last little garden" he walked in with his wife and son at St. Nazaire, just before going on board ship to sail to America — a garden with "a geometrical design which no doubt I could easily fill in with the colors of plausible flowers."

What is most fascinating about the memory art of *Speak, Memory* is that things long dead and vanished in the past come fully to life precisely by being placed within a series of frames, by being "reduced" or "fixed" in a pattern, by being subdued to imagery and artifice. If memory speaks it speaks visually, beckoning through a window, and we are left in the face of this happy mystery to reflect that the charmed life possessed by objects, persons, and places that time has consumed owes nothing to the prison house of temporality and everything to the art by which they have been evoked out of the "contiguous world" that Nabokov has opened the windows of his figures and images upon.

Collectors — of butterflies and cold nests — are often solitary men. But *Speak, Memory*, established upon the intuition of man's ineluctable solitude, terminates, through a happy inconsistency, in communion. Its last chapter, addressed to Nabokov's own wife and recollecting the birth and infancy of Dmitri, celebrates nothing less than a happy marriage. This marriage is the single gift out of the past which needs no re-creation in art. Nabokov says, "I must know where I stand, where you and my son stand"; and where he stands, in the now of affectionate concern to which the book returns from its exploration of the past, is upon "mortal love." All or nearly all of Nabokov's books are dedicated to his wife Véra, whose name in Russian is also the word for faith, belief, religion, and trust. Let us turn now to his novels proper to see what happens to his intuition of man's imprisonment in consciousness and time, his theme of transcendence through image making, and his faith in mortal marital love as he creates over a period of more than forty years a body of work in fiction which is like no other writer's anywhere in our part of the twentieth century.

There are now available in English eight Nabokov novels originally composed in Russian and six composed in English. Before giving extended consideration to four of these books — my choices reflect factors of personal taste, a sense of where the inner dialectic of Nabokov's artistic vision is most significantly at work, and a keen sense of the space limits of the pamphlet form — I have a particular point to make about all his novels that can best be clarified through briefer discussion of a fairly large number of them.

The point is this: Nabokov's novels are never direct imitations of life. Invariably, they are imitations of imitations of life. A Nabokov novel does not begin with or issue from a selection of experience with concomitant selection of a governing point of view. Rather, it issues from the deliberate selection of a formal narrative type or structure, occasionally from selection of nonfictional narrative forms such as the biography, and, just once, from selection of the non-narrative form of scholarly commentary and emendation. Nabokov is a spirited and learned parodist of prose forms accumulated through the evolution of literary history in the West, yet his impulses to parody are not pedantic or frivolous; nor do they constitute acts of aggression against either literary history or literary art. Rather, he has a sophisticated and true awareness of how forms of literary art and organization are forms of consciousness au fond, of how a given type of narrative frames a definite perspective on experience. One kind of narrative, to change the metaphor, fences out—in terms of characterization, angle of narration, the representation of place or of societal data, the ordering of events, the tone and pace of narration, and so forth — one entire set of human possibilities while fencing in some other set. To put this oversimply, a gothic romance will usually eschew a hard, dry narrative tone, while a novel cast in the form of a confession will not employ the viewpoint of omniscience. A crime novel will usually be more logically ordered with respect to plot than a metaphysical fantasy emphasizing enigmatic aspects of reality. A *Bildungsroman* will stress the accumulating experience and viewpoint of one central character over that of other characters, and a ghost story, unless it is merely a debunking of the supernatural, will use supernatural material as though apparitions are real.

Nabokov uses all the types I have mentioned and others as well with full awareness of what each ordinarily can and cannot be made to do. Precisely because he is so aware he often introduces twists and drastic modifications, even sometimes breeds type with type, working somewhat on the analogy of the gifted laboratory experimenter who moves out from the known to the unknown by viewing the materials of his experiment from unexpected angles and combining them in new ways. It is a highly conscious process. Nabokov has nothing but contempt for the concept of simple sincerity in art, which he equates with a fatuous willingness to pour old spoiled wine into leaky bottles. He is, for example, one of the great originators in contemporary letters of that fictional hybrid called black comedy. Black comedy in his hands is just such a product of scrupulously supervised crossbreeding as no artistic practice or critical method founded upon moralistic notions of the sincere in art could have created or predicted.

King, Queen, Knave (1928), second earliest of his novels to receive English translation, conforms to the fictional type that centers on a young man of humble provincial origins who seeks social and commercial advancement in the city, only to become corrupted there and lapse back into a deeper obscurity. An obvious exemplar, to which Nabokov obliquely refers in a foreword written for the English translation of 1968, is Dreiser's *An American Tragedy*; but Nabokov's detached, deliberately diagrammatic treatment of his central characters — Dreyer, a Berlin department store owner, Martha, his unfaithful and treacherous wife, and knavish Franz, his dull, gullible, and ultimately treacherous nephew — reduces the central intrigue, a scheme to murder Dreyer that is attempted and bungled by the wife and nephew, to a kind of puppet show acted out by mannequinlike creatures whose relationships and conflicts can be fully specified by the cipher language of a game of cards: K (unwittingly) against QKn with a mysterious trump card of accident introduced at the last moment to give the game to K. *King, Queen, Knave*, by taking the nature out of Dreiserian (and Flaubertian) naturalism, exposes the bare bones of naturalistic contrivance. It also exposes the emptiness and sterility of an "advanced" German bourgeois milieu where people live lives of blank desperation in houses designed, decorated, and furnished according to the rational, geometric canons of the Bauhaus and the Dutch *De Stijl* movements.

The Eye (1930) is a novella belonging to the category of ghost story. An unhappy, self-obsessed young Russian named Smurov shoots himself because he is unlucky in love, is uncertain of his true nature, and imagines himself despised by various Russian expatriates frequenting a certain lodging house in Berlin. He then returns as a ghostly spy and wanders through the minds of the people who had spurned him in life, taking note of the several wholly distinct and incompatible versions of his own identity which different

18

minds go on entertaining. At the end it appears that he is not dead after all, nor is the original mystery about the nature of "the true Smurov" cleared up to either his or the reader's satisfaction. This abiding mystery is a lively and illuminating way of pointing to the problems of identity created by the stance of extreme self-consciousness. *The Eye* is, at once, a comic investigation of late adolescent self-concern, the portrait of a shy, autistic, and endearing young man who ought to take up writing as a strategy for self-encounter, a fable about the vocation of the imagining and remarking artist and the price he pays in isolation and self-effacement for his special kind of awareness, and, finally, perhaps an early self-portrait of the artist who wrote it.

The Defense (also 1930) is the first of several novels which invent extraordinary variations on the imaginary biography. When Nabokov has this type in hand his central character is always remarkable and usually a genius. Moreover, the author nearly always chooses to emphasize the deep solitude and the inevitable estrangement from other people that represent the price exacted by destiny for the gift of high imaginative or intellectual powers. Most of Nabokov's central characters are unrepentant individualists; his geniuses are merely the extreme limit of the general case.

Luzhin, the Russian-born hero of *The Defense*, is a forlorn, inarticulate, and physically graceless chess genius, a sort of *idiot savant* of the international tournament circuit. After a wretched boyhood and a lonely adult career it becomes his fate to fall in love (with a good woman who loves him in return) when it is too late, when his mind has been taken over by a paranoid affliction which resolves the issues, projects, and challenges of his daily life into a series of chess moves based upon an unwinnable defensive strategy. What Nabokov calls "chess effects" are worked into the narrative throughout, reaching a climax in the last scene — one of the great tours de force in all of Nabokov's fiction. Here Luzhin, the king at check in his own apartment, the rooms and corridors of which appear to him under the aspect of the game he is forced to play and cannot win, tries to break out of the entrapment by bursting through the frosted white square of the bathroom window. But he falls to his death into a chasm of "dark and pale squares" which show him "exactly what kind of eternity was obligingly and inexorably spread out before him."

Nabokov's preface to the English translation of *The Defense*, published in 1964, appears to hint that Luzhin's losing moves are based on an actual historic match, the "Immortal Game" played between L. Kieseritsky and A. Anderssen during a London tournament of masters in 1851. Although in *Speak, Memory* he characterizes his hobby of composing chess problems as a "beautiful, complex and sterile art" there is nothing bloodless about the "combinational" artistry of *The Defense*, and Luzhin himself, in his gentleness, profound introversion, and total incapacity for coping with the "real world," remains one of Nabokov's most touching and lovingly drawn characterizations. For Nabokov the chessboard appears as "a system of stresses and abysses," possessed of the same three-dimensional qualities and fatal choices as life itself. By the same token, life in Nabokov's novels can sometimes appear, as it certainly does in *The Defense*, to be a three-dimensional chess game the issue of which is clouded by a terrible, teasing question: are men the players at the board or are they merely the pawns and other pieces of the game? And if the latter, who controls the play?

John Shade, the "preterist" poet in *Pale Fire*, opts for the second theory and finds solace in the notion that the life he does not control becomes endurable through his contemplative appreciation of its intricate "web of sense":

> Yes! It sufficed that I in life could find
> Some kind of link-and-bobolink, some kind
> Of correlated pattern in the game,

> Plexed artistry, and something of the same
> Pleasure in it as they who played it found.

But it is doubtful that Shade could respond with unqualified appreciation to the sequence of "topsyturvical coincidence" that led to his own violent death, and there are Nabokov novels which address the clouded issue of human fate and freedom with anything but equanimity. Two of these are perhaps best treated in close proximity because they are both novels about "actual" imprisonment and oppression at the hands — under the heel rather — of political state power.

Invitation to a Beheading (1938) follows the fictional type of metaphysical fantasy with political overtones that we are familiar with from the works of Franz Kafka. One can believe Nabokov's disclaimer of any knowledge of Kafka at the time of its composition around 1934, and still remain free to surmise that the book does respond imaginatively to certain grotesque and awful features of modern totalitarianism that Kafka's fiction had prophetically anticipated. The hero, Cincinnatus C., is sequestered in a solitary cell within a castle fortress and awaits execution by beheading. His crime, called "gnostical turpitude" in the bill of indictment against him, is to have remained an individual, thinking his own thoughts and reflecting on the world in his own way. He has no ally within the prison, unless it is Emmie, the jailer's child, who appears mysteriously within his cell, shows him enigmatic stick drawings which appear to diagram an escape route, and leads him, as if in a cruelly deceptive dream, through a maze of corridors that return him finally to his own cell. He is tricked at every turn: the other "prisoner" who tunnels through his cell wall turns out to be his executioner; his unfaithful wife sides with his tormentors; even the window high on one wall through which he longs to look out upon the "Tamara Gardens," a paradisal place where "we used to roam

and hide" in childhood, is a painted fake complete with a clock-
work spider spinning a synthetic web.

What is demanded of Cincinnatus before his beheading is something even worse than his confession to crimes he has not commit-
ted. It is complete, self-degrading cooperation in his own undoing.
The regime, farcical in its inefficiency and the downright clownish-
ness of its officials, maintains itself on a single obscene and inhuman
principle, that of collaboration. In securing Cincinnatus' conviction the defense attorney has collaborated with the prosecutor and
the judge with both. At the ultimate reach of infamy the prisoner
is expected to waltz with the jailer, compliment the prison governor
on the excellence of the prison accommodation, admire the axe-
man for his expertise, and post to his decapitation as if honored by
an Invitation to the Dance. Declining the invitation, Cincinnatus
resists quietly to the end. Yet it is just this bizarre feature of the
wholly corrupt prison world of *Invitation* that evokes direct parallels with the actual history of modern totalitarian states. Whether
we think of the ritualistic public confessions of the Moscow treason
trials in the 1930's or of the Nazi death camps in the 1940's, where
prisoners were encouraged to compete for the privilege of dying
last by helping the guards to torture and kill their fellow prisoners,
we are contemplating the same perversion of the collaborative principle.

Despite these historical parallels, *Invitation to a Beheading* is
scarcely a work of fictional realism. The temporal setting is future — almost no — time; the fortress and the adjacent town, with
its winding streets, public fountain and statues, the Tamara Gardens and the woodland beyond, seem to belong to the vaguely
medieval world of central European folklore rather than to the
world we know. By contrast, *Bend Sinister* (1947), characterized by
Nabokov as having "stylistic links" to *Invitation*, comes much
closer to the type of the overtly political novel. In 1947 the small

22

nations of Eastern Europe were bending left under pressure from the U.S.S.R. *Bend Sinister*, for all its qualities of fantasy and its many passages which hint that the oppressions suffered by its main characters reflect universal conditions, depicts a turning away from individual freedoms toward an imposed collectivism that closely resembles what was happening in such countries as Poland, Bulgaria, Hungary, Rumania, and Czechoslovakia during the immediate postwar period.

Bend Sinister, written in English, is perhaps Nabokov's only morbid book. Its hero, Adam Krug, a distinguished philosopher and university professor in a nameless country whose inhabitants speak a Slavic language of sorts, sees his beloved wife succumb to illness within the first few pages. Better for Krug to have died with her in view of what is to come. The country has been taken over by a revolutionary clique preaching perfect equality but employing totalitarian methods of terror and under the control of a dictator called Paduk — the Toad. Paduk, who is an old schoolfellow of Krug's, the sadistic bully of the play yard, and whose name is a virtual anagram of the Russian *upadok*, signifying decay, decline, degeneration, wants Krug broken into conformity so that less prominent citizens of the country will not be inspired by Krug's notorious individualism to go on thinking thoughts of their own.

The means taken to break him are awful and yet perfectly familiar to anyone who has read the newspapers during the past three or four decades. Krug is summoned to a blandishing and threatening interview with the Toad himself, "clothed from carbuncle to bunion in field gray," his eyes those "of a fish in a neglected aquarium." When the tactic is unsuccessful, the state apparatus of terror takes over. Krug is driven from the university and subjected to harassment and spying by the police. His only son, David, upon whom Krug lavishes the affection of a grief-stricken widower as well as a doting father, is stolen from him, tortured, and then murdered. Finally, Krug is put into solitary confinement after having been shown on film the particulars of his son's fate.

Both *Invitation to a Beheading* and *Bend Sinister*, to the extent that they are concerned with politics and society, reflect a bottomless pessimism about politics and the social process in our time. While reading these books one keeps remembering that their author was driven into exile and saw his father killed because of "politics" and that the absolute individualism of Nabokov's world view tends to deny him the consolation of belief that any agency, operating in or beyond history, will eventually redeem the sufferings inflicted on innocent and decent people by savage and incompetent ideologues and power brokers in this century. Both books end with spectacular Nabokovian *coups de théâtre* the significance of which remains perfectly equivocal. At the moment of his beheading, Cincinnatus finds that he is on his feet and walking freely through collapsing and disintegrating bits of stage scenery, "in that direction where, to judge by the voices, stood beings akin to him." And at the moment when Krug, in prison, is about to awaken to the "hideous misfortune" of his lot, Nabokov tells us *in propria persona* that "I felt a pang of pity for Adam and slid towards him along an inclined beam of pale light — causing instantaneous madness, but at least saving him from the senseless agony of his logical fate." In each case, especially in the second, the author plays God, arriving from beyond the prisoning "form" (logical and teleological) of the story to help the helpless character. But there is nothing in Nabokov's sense of the human plight as a whole to which these acts of compassionate intervention provide an analogy. There is no God of compassion or redemption in the universe at large who will do for "Adam" what the author Nabokov does for his characters by means of a merely ironic, and in some sense despairing, trick of fiction.

After thus illustrating my point about the way Nabokov employs, modifies, and reanimates various narrative structures or types — the way in which his books are artful imitations of imitations — I want now to consider in more depth the several books in the Nabokov canon of fiction to which one finds oneself returning frequently; the books which express most hauntingly and richly his deepest sense of life; which in particular represent the core of permanence in his work, or, rather, the permanent addition he has made to the house of fiction in our time.

I have in mind four novels — two from the 1930's originally written in Russian, two from the 1950's and 1960's originally written in English — which arrange themselves across the language barrier and the time gap as two related pairings. The first pair consists of *Kamera Obskura* (1933) — titled *Camera Obscura* in its first translated version (London, 1936) but retitled *Laughter in the Dark* in its revised American translation of 1938, which I am following here — and *Lolita* (1955). These are intimately related as melodramas of audacious metaphysical crime centering upon the theme of the "nymphet." The second pair consists of *Dar* (1938; 1952), translated as *The Gift* in 1963, and *Pale Fire* (1962). The first is a book about a young poet which uses the framing devices of imaginary biography and the *Künstlerroman* to explore the themes of poetic art, Russian literary culture, and young love. The second is a book about an old poet which uses the devices of scholarly commentary, imaginary autobiography, and poetry itself to explore the themes of poetic art, of the irredeemability of time past, and of human solitude in counterpoise with wedded love.

Laughter in the Dark and *Lolita* differ tremendously in nearly all respects, not least in the degree of self-awareness of their chief characters, the suggestively named Albinus and the self-designated "Humbert Humbert." Yet Albinus and Humbert stand closer together in a crucially important respect than any other two characters in Nabokov. Both are possessed by a thirst for the infinite, suf-

fer from the metaphysical obsession traditionally named the "de-
sire and pursuit of the whole." Further, both have received a true
intuition that the route to the infinite is through attachment to an
adorable image or eidolon, yet both blunder, perversely and fatally,
by haplessly confounding the image with its illusory reflection or
echo in the flesh of a child-woman. The consequence is that they
fall, into an enslavement entailing their torture and mockery by
demonic men, artists themselves, who as film makers are in the
business of degrading images, who as nemeses raised by the obses-
sions of their victims have (and delight in) the task of punishing
Albinus and Humbert for their idolatrous passions.

Literally, "camera obscura" means "dark chamber." More com-
prehensively, a camera obscura is any dark chamber including pho-
tographic cameras, darkened cinema palaces, a prison cell, and, for
Nabokov, the cranial cell behind the eyes wherein imprisoned
consciousness languishes, with a lens or opening through which an
image may be projected in "natural" colors onto a receptive surface. Nabokov's choice of the camera obscura as a guiding metaphor in his account of Albinus' dismal fate becomes perfectly
logical and appropriate, given his powerfully visual imagination,
his notion of images as windows and apertures, his notion of man
as a prisoner languishing within walls of time and contingency, and
his conviction that imagination is the faculty of consciousness
which attempts to spy beyond the prison walls through image making. Albinus, an art dealer and connoisseur, sins through the eyes,
by entering a darkened motion picture house and glimpsing there
something deeply illicit and corrupt which he mistakes for a vision
of human felicity. He is led on and on into deeper and darker
mistaking until he receives the appropriate punishment for his
misuse of the faculty of vision. Physically blinded, morally de-
graded, mocked, confined, and at last murdered by his vicious

26

young mistress, he is the object of that awful laughter in the dark made mention of in the American translation's title.

Laughter in the Dark makes darkly ironic play with the "optical" themes of art connoisseurship, painting and caricature, film making, life modeling, and film stardom in conjunction with a melodramatic plot recalling the famous German film *Die Blaue Engel* to suggest that, whereas true art is a way of seeing truly in darkness, attachment to false images leads only to a deeper benightedness and closer confinement.

Albinus, a prosperous Berlin art dealer possessed of a genuine "passion for art" and a bourgeois German "happy family" reaches that familiar critical point in early middle age when a man of his type may fall prey to a malaise of uneasiness and dissatisfaction whose causes are half spiritual and half sexual. He thinks of launching new art projects and dreams of amatory adventures with pretty young girls that would restore to his life a dimension of erotic intensity missing from his marriage. The new art project takes shape from an idle habit he has fallen into of "having this or that Old Master sign landscapes and faces which he, Albinus, came across in real life: it turned his existence into a fine picture gallery — delightful fakes, all of them." He is interested in the new popular art of the movies and conceives the clever, possibly profitable scheme of producing cartoons which will animate a famous painting by one of the Dutch Old Masters like Brueghel and give the figures in the static picture a continuing life through an entire episode. At the beginning it would be something simple, "a stained window coming to life," yet to begin at all he needs a collaborator combining knowledge of art with skill as an animated cartoonist. Unfortunately, the man for the job, one Axel Rex, a gifted graphic artist and caricaturist, is away in America drawing newspaper cartoons.

Albinus writes to Rex who warms to the scheme and asks for

large advances of money to undertake the work. Meanwhile Albinus wanders one day into a movie house called the Argus and sees in the dark the outline of his fate: "the melting outline of a cheek which looked as though it were painted by a great artist against a rich dark background." The possessor of the cheek, an usherette named Margot Peters, who is about seventeen and looks even younger, responds to Albinus' tentative advances. He begins an affair with her that soon becomes wretchedly obsessive for him and that scandalizes his family and friends and leads to the break-up of his marriage.

To this point, we can say that Albinus has indeed confused the passions appropriate to art and to life and is punished for it. But the book to this point has barely begun and the aftermath has little relevance to this merely cautionary moral. In becoming involved with Margot and with Rex, Albinus has crossed an invisible line into an absolutely sinister world organized as a conspiracy against him, a world of complete deception where the animate images of art and pseudo-art are manipulated by a master craftsman in the art of evildoing. To begin with, Margot, the tough, amoral, mindless slum child, turns out to be entirely a creature of the camera-obscura world. She has been first an artist's model posing for life classes in an art school, next the model and mistress of Axel Rex before his American sojourn, and her career as usherette is intended to be merely a stopover on the way to becoming a screen star. In the end she indeed becomes as a motion picture actress that "silver ghost of romance" — impalpable, depthless, talentless, soulless, the net product of advertising, publicity, and opportunistic manipulation — and, ironically enough, the human creature redefined as sheer artful image that Albinus had gone seeking when he began to frequent movie houses and sign real faces with the signatures of Old Masters.

It is a shattering coincidence that Margot should have been connected with Axel even before Albinus met her, although it is no surprise that she joins forces with him to manipulate and then destroy Albinus after Axel's return. Nabokov invariably uses such coincidences, plays with such loaded dice, in order to draw the reader away from his "realistic" expectations and to introduce him to a world where fate has little to do with character and functions like a conspiracy whose ultimate aim, as in the delusional systems of paranoiacs, is never actually made clear. Axel is a real artist of considerable talent who has made a career of faking pictures and drawing vicious caricatures, and who believes "that everything . . . in the domain of art . . . was only a more or less clever trick." He is a real confidence man too, with the practical aim of separating Albinus from his money. But his taste for the confidence game goes far beyond the practical. He sees himself as a "stage manager" who can be counted on to arrange the "roaring comedy" of Albinus' miseries and the kind of manager he "had in view was an elusive, double, triple, self-reflecting magic Proteus of a phantom, the shadow of many-colored glass balls flying in a curve, the ghost of a juggler on a shimmering curtain."

Here the stage manager melts into the performer, with Margot also on stage (or screen) to assist the clever magician or evil Magus in his show. Throughout the book Margot has the particular assignment, after leading Albinus on, of closing him in. She is always shutting doors on him and eventually seals him into permanent blindness as the result of an auto accident for which she is actually responsible. The phantom role comes to full flower for Axel when Albinus, after he has been blinded, takes a house in Switzerland and lives there alone — he imagines — with his adored Margot. In fact Axel is also in the house, a silent presence, going naked and making love to Margot under Albinus' very nose. He likes to watch Margot make faces of "comic" disgust when Albinus, thinking they are alone, embraces the girl tenderly. He will touch the blind man

29

gently with the tips of his bare toes and dissolves in silent laughter when Albinus assumes that it is Margot's caressing touch. And he will sit close to him for hours until the blind man, sensing a presence near him, reaches out, whereupon Axel gleefully moves back out of reach. At this time Albinus is a man in ruins with most of his money gone; so the impulse to mischief which continues to drive Axel and Margot really does constitute a "motiveless malignity." It is a "comic" performance by devils playing "disinterestedly," i.e., for love of their "art," to an audience of one who cannot see.

Eventually Albinus learns what has been going on from his decent brother-in-law, Paul. He takes refuge in Paul's Berlin house and on a certain day manages to entrap Margot in the drawing room of the old family apartment, which she is busily looting of the art objects he had collected during his career as a connoisseur. He is armed and tries to sense where she is so that he can kill her. Their grim struggle, conducted behind closed doors and for him wholly in darkness, results in his own death when Margot grabs the revolver and shoots him. The final paragraphs, written as directions for a film or stage scene, stress that the door of the drawing room is now open and "the door leading from the hall to the landing is wide open, too." As we have seen with *Invitation to a Beheading*, physical death is the opening into freedom for the doomed, betrayed prisoner, although neither book can follow the released man through that opening.

Much of *Laughter in the Dark* is composed in Nabokov's sprightliest and most playful vein. But to complain of the author's apparent callousness to the sufferings of his central character is to miss the important point. Albinus' "passion for art" which betrays him into a realm of sexual and social pathology really does contain "immortal longings" with which the author has complete sympathy. But the author understands, as Albinus does not, that the beguiling images and forms beckoning in the murk of human reality are for seeing and not for possessing — an insight available to the true artist though not to the connoisseur with his checkbook and collections. "Albinus' speciality had been his passion for art; his most brilliant discovery had been Margot. But now . . . it was as though she had returned to the darkness of the little cinema from which he had once withdrawn her." On his way into the Argus Cinema Albinus had noticed a poster showing "a man looking up at a window framing a child in a nightshirt." This representation, which will reappear as an imagistic theme in *Lolita*, scrupulously balances an idea of aspiration toward something purely beautiful with the pathology of voyeurism and sexual perversion. It is also a warning which Albinus cannot read or heed because he is so mad for form that he will not distinguish between form and its replica or model: "Now, the vision of the promised kiss filled him with such ecstasy that it seemed hardly possible it could be still further intensified. And yet beyond it, down a vista of mirrors, there was still to be reached the dim white form of her body, that very form which art students had sketched so conscientiously and so badly."

Lolita's unique appropriation of the American landscape, its comic and sinister play with American social institutions and roles and their deep-lying anomie, the wit and beauty of its endlessly inventive narrative style, coming in the midst of a bad decade for American fiction, fell upon our literary scene like a small hurricane ("Hurricane Lolita"!). Fifteen years later criticism was just beginning to take the measure of the book. When the critical history of the American novel in the 1960's and 1970's is written, *Lolita*'s presence and influence in that history will be major and central. *Lolita* killed fictional naturalism, already moribund, with one merciful blow. More important, it nerved a new generation of writers to meet the drastic and fantastic realities of American life with a countering imaginative fierceness and boldness. Our most interesting recent writers, from Barth to Burroughs, from Thomas Berger to Thomas Pynchon, owe more to Nabokov, to the Nabokov of *Lolita* especially, than to any other contemporary figure, American or foreign.

In terms of Nabokov's own work *Lolita* has a similar centrality and prominence. In it he comes to final accommodation with the nymphet theme, which had been echoing and reechoing in his work for decades, and links the theme lucidly to the master themes of nostalgia (or preterism) and of imagination which form the principal coordinates of his entire created world. Unlike Albinus, who never understands what he is doing, Humbert Humbert, conducting his own defense — "O ladies and gentlemen of the jury" — and, as critics often fail to note, his own prosecution, comes to know fully what he has done and is responsible for. He is in all of Nabokov's fiction the supremely conscious individualist, the wholly confident manipulator of the bewildering variety of his roles, and in this confidence reflects Nabokov's own masterly grasp of his most complex creation in character.

Nabokov has remarked of Humbert that although he went straight and properly to hell after the guards found him dead of a coronary in his cell, where he awaited trial for the slaying of Quilty, the man who had taken Lolita from him, Humbert may be allowed the privilege of returning to earth for one day each year. On that day one might expect him to haunt the environs of the little mining town in the American West, mentioned in the book's concluding pages, "that lay at my feet, in a fold of the valley," from which rose "the melody of children at play." Here it was that the bestial and enchanted hunter of nymphets rejoined the human race when he at last "knew that the hopelessly poignant thing was not Lolita's absence from my side, but the absence of her voice from that concord." And if we are inclined to suspect his sentiments here there is another late episode which indicates the same belated conversion. Lolita has written him after years of silence and absence to say she is married, pregnant, and in need of money. He finds her in a shack in "Coalmont," eight hundred miles from New York City, big-bellied, worn out at seventeen, and he wants to steal her away again or kill her if she will not come. But then he realizes that he loves her *as she is*, not merely as the echo or memory "of the nymphet I had rolled myself upon with such cries in the past . . . Thank God it was not that echo alone that I worshiped." The "echo" of course points to the "eidolon" he had pursued lifelong, spying into "jewel-bright" windows and depraving little girls because the print of sexual characteristics was still so faintly impressed upon their childish bodies that he could pretend when savaging them that he was cleaving to a pure form and recapturing the lost Edenic time he had spent in childhood with "Annabel Lee." Lolita is spectacularly and maturely pregnant, no longer the "Idolores" of his original quest. He earns his overnight pass from hell by loving her and leaving her — several thousand dollars richer — going off to hunt down and kill the "rival devil," Quilty, whose taste for sexual frolics with children, as with dwarfs, is an ordinary piece of psychopathy lacking transcendental overtones.

But even at Coalmont Humbert does not relinquish his habit of imaginary role playing. He casts the scene as Don José's final confrontation with Carmen ("*Changeons de vie, ma Carmen*," etc.) and says goodbye to his "American sweet immortal dead love," who has just made him understand for the first time that "the past was the past," under the aspect of a fat tenor from grand opera. One of the joys of *Lolita* is Humbert's role playing. Just as the book as a whole encapsulates and parodies every literary confession of a great sinner from St. Augustine to Sade, Rousseau, and Stavrogin, so do Humbert's roles introduce a rich variety of imaginative frames and thematic aspects through which the book's action may be viewed.

To touch very lightly on this matter, consider the following. When Lolita is Bee or Beatrice, Humbert is Dante and the evoked mode is an inversion of "divine comedy" (hellish comedy?). When she is "Dolores Disparu," Humbert is Proust's Marcel lamenting the vanished Albertine and the mode is Proustian speculation about the enigmas of time and memory. When she is Vee (Virginia Clem), Humbert is Edgar Allan Poe and the frame is artist's biography in the era of "romantic agony." When she merges with "Annabel" Humbert is the child narrator of Poe's famous poem. And when Humbert, fleeing the mysterious Aztec red convertible with Lolita through the American night, murmurs *"lente, lente, currite noctis equi,"* Humbert is Faustus, Lolita is both Helen and Gretchen, and the mode, if not the mood, is that of Marlowe's tragic morality play. Also there are Humbert's less literary roles, each played to the hilt: the spy and voyeur ("Humbert Humbert — two eyes burning in the dark"), the European gentleman with a "past," the family friend, the husband and mature lover, the "stepfather" concerned to guard his little charge safely through the toils of teendom, the private investigator, the madman, the devil slayer ("guilty of killing Quilty"), and, finally and throughout, the pleader-prosecutor at heaven's bar — "O winged gentlemen!"

Nabokov's own cryptic key to *Lolita* was given in a 1956 "Postscript" to the first American edition. There he said the idea came to him in Paris in 1938, during an attack of neuralgia and after reading a "pointless" newspaper story about a scientist who attempted to teach an ape to draw. The ape did produce a drawing, but it was only of the bars of its cage. Humbert, that greatly talented ape, attempts a break-out, an act of transcendence, through his mad and cruel pursuit of the eidolon, incarnate in little Dolores Haze, Lolita, but he merely succeeds in confirming his confinement in matter, in the grossly sensual self, in vice and in time. One can add to this very little, except perhaps — since *Lolita* is already an assured American classic — a suggestion of how the book reverberates through our specifically American historic culture.

The core element of Humbert's sexual perversity, arch-romanticism, and derangement is an attitude toward time which may remind us of other eccentric or deranged heroes of American fiction. Humbert is fixated on the past — on his childhood love affair with "Annabel Lee" — and his pursuit, seduction, and enslavement of Dolores Haze are an attempt to reinstate in the present and preserve into the future what was irretrievably lost in the past. The expensiveness of indulgence in this illusion is very great: it costs no less than the wrecking of a child's life, as Humbert finally admits after abandoning his corrupt rationalizations concerning the natural depravity and sexual precocity of American little girls. Humbert and his time problem are summed up on the final page of *The Great Gatsby*, from which I quoted at the onset of this essay, and in a number of other classic American texts.

But how can this vile European stand in for an archetypal American? There is really no problem. America, as a "brand new, mad new dream world where everything [is] permissible," is Europe's dream of itself according to the romantic error that past time is retrievable. Emerson, Whitman, and Hart Crane might have approved Humbert's thought, if not his exact words and their appalling application. We are all Europeans when we dream that dangerous, beguiling, ever-so-American dream.

These speculations can be pushed a bit further under the general rubric of fate, freedom, and America. *Lolita*, because it is heavy with fate, would seem to present a situation in which the margin of freedom which interests us in fictional characters, particularly in the characters appearing in modern books, has diminished virtually to nothing. For instance, Humbert is obsessed, Lolita is enslaved, Charlotte Haze is totally duped, and a character like Quilty is the slave of his sinister vices. Add in fate as the "synchronizing phantom" arranging happenstance and coincidence upon wholly mysterious principles and freedom disappears altogether from the book. From another angle, there is freedom in *Lolita* of a rather awful sort. Humbert is free, unencumbered with compunction before his "conversion." Through most of the book he has the freedom of his viciousness, as does Quilty. Humbert's actions take place at a point in history when traditional sanctions have lapsed or at least loosened, and there would be very little consensus of judgment against his deeds from the "enlightened" sector of the community, apart from agreement that he is psychologically "disturbed." This in effect forgives and forgets by understanding or claiming to.

Dolores Haze also is free in a sense, in that the nature of contemporary American "suburban" culture ties her to nothing, asks nothing of her, presents her with nothing. What is she? A junior consumer, of comic books and bubble gum, a "starlet" with a thirst for cheap films and Coke. There is a great vacancy in and around her, a voidness and loneliness only partly created by Humbert's machinations. This vacancy is cultural in the first instance, American.

For Europe, as first de Toqueville and then D. H. Lawrence have expounded, America has figured as the place beyond cabined and confined traditions and sanctions. It has been the place where time itself might be redeemed, where the dream of a new Eden, of a second life, could be realized. Naturally, there has been a dark, pathological side to this. America has been the place indubitably attractive to great mischief makers, psychopaths, men on the run, unclubable and violent persons, con men. Humbert lives on the dark side of the American freedom I am describing. There is some truth in the statement that what drove Humbert to America was his vice and the hope of satisfying it in the land of opportunity. And there is also some truth in the idea that the history of Lolita, who died in childbed in a town of the "remotest Northwest" on her way to Alaska, the last American frontier, expresses the final decadence of that European myth which we call the American Dream.

Nabokov has called *The Gift* "the best, the most nostalgic of my Russian novels." It is also, even in the excellent English translation of 1963, the least accessible of Nabokov's major works to the general English-speaking reader. As a *Künstlerroman* celebrating the life of literature and the literary life it tells the story of a young Russian émigré poet and critic named Fyodor Godunov-Cherdyntsev discovering his artistic powers and finding love as well over a three-year period in Berlin during the mid-1920's. But *The Gift* is also a complex, playful, and creative work of literary criticism oriented toward the pre-Soviet Russian cultural tradition and aimed as a sidelong polemic against certain dubious values obtaining among literary and cultural pundits of the Russian émigré community in Western Europe. Lacking close knowledge of the literally dozens of minor and major Russian writers the book alludes to, and of the many issues and personalities from the expatriate cultural scene at which the book takes a fling, the reader may well feel he should acquire, along with a mastery of Russian literature, history, and the language, that ideal insomnia which Joyce recommended to the ideal reader of *Finnegans Wake*.

Nevertheless, the main focus of Nabokov's revaluation of tradition is quite clear. Centering his attack on the liberal and progressive critic and novelist N. G. Chernyshevski, he tasks the progressive wing of nineteenth-century Russian culture, and by implication the liberal wing of the émigré community, with a confusion of values whereby "enlightened" writers of small talent have been overpraised at the expense of better writers possessing unacceptable social and political views. For Nabokov and for Fyodor, the great tradition begins in Pushkin and is passed down through a select few poets and prose writers whose social views, radical or conservative, are of no bearing whatsoever. It is a tradition and dialogue of artists constituting the supreme gift the Russian literary genius and language have to offer, a gift which Fyodor aspires to receive, through an utmost effort of critical understanding, to share in to the limit of his developing artistic powers, and to pass on uncompromised whether or not he ever has the good fortune to return to a Russia in which a poet like himself can once again carry on serious work.

The Gift is arranged in five big chapters and each chapter advances Fyodor's personal history while simultaneously undertaking assessments and recapitulations of Russian art. In the early chapters Fyodor works at his own poetry, finds ways of supporting himself in a city whose people and their civic ways interest him not in the slightest, meets and begins courting a delightful and sensitive Russian girl named Zina Mertz whose vulgar stepfather is Fyodor's landlord. A mysterious poet-critic named Koncheyev appears and disappears at intervals. In rapid, allusive dialogue Fyodor and this imaginary alter ego, with whom Fyodor is always in essential agreement about artistic values, work out their aesthetic credo and dismiss from contention all those mystics, progressives, and poetasters who, in their arrogantly youthful view, appear as excrescences on the brilliant surface of Russian literature. Chapter Two, which might be called the book of the father, shows Fyodor absorbed in biographical and critical studies of his poetic master, Pushkin, while also collecting information about the career of his fleshly father, a great naturalist-scientist who had disappeared at the time of the Bolshevik Revolution on his way back from one of his long expeditions in Central Asia. Fyodor's largely fictional reconstructions of these journeys, written under the stylistic influence of Pushkin and filled with exotic yet scientifically exact descriptions of the plants, butterflies, and landscapes encountered en route, form one of Nabokov's most marvelous achievements in prose.

In Chapter Three Fyodor explores deeper into questions of the creative process in poetry, works out the important connections between the art of Pushkin and what is worth cherishing in later

Russian verse, and begins research and writing for a "critical" biography of Chernyshevski. Chapter Four is in its entirety a very
funny yet mainly accurate and learned short biography of Chernyshevski. It introduces an imaginary authority named Strannolyub-
ski (Strangelove?) who reports that during Chernyshevski's Siberian
exile "once an eagle appeared in his yard . . . It had come to peck
at his liver but did not recognize Prometheus in him." Nabokov's
(and Fyodor's) purpose is to expose Chernyshevski as the false Prometheus of Russian tradition, a savant whose sincere good inten-
tions and abundant sufferings in the cause of righteousness cannot
excuse the dullness, dogmatism, and anti-aesthetic bias of his judg-
ments and influence.

Chapter Four, which might be called the book of the false father,
forms the polemical climax of *The Gift*. If one aim of the work has
been to locate and consolidate the great tradition of Russian writing the corollary aim has been to expose an anti-tradition incarnate
in social critics of the Chernyshevskian school whom Nabokov in-
sists on seeing not only as the promulgators of a sound tradition of
reformism and social concern but also as responsible for their own
and others' bad writing, for a misappropriation of the Russian
Hegelian tradition leading to dogmatic Marxist-Leninism, and,
finally, for the worst excesses of Soviet philistinism in the cultural
sphere.

Chapter Four gave great offense to critics and progressives of the
émigré world, so much so that it was not printed as part of the
book until 1952. Chapter Five, anticipating this reaction, presents
excerpts from imaginary book reviews of Chapter Four. Nabokov
faithfully renders the style and bias of numerous literary pundits,
including several who write from a politically reactionary or fanati-
cally religious point of view. But the best review, a sympathetic
one, is contributed by "Koncheyev," who reappears just when he is
needed to aid the beleaguered and beset Fyodor in his "heretical"

undertakings: "[Koncheyev] began by drawing a picture of flight during an invasion or an earthquake, when the escapers carry away with them everything that they can lay hands on, someone being sure to burden himself with a large, framed portrait of some long-forgotten relatives. 'Just such a portrait,' wrote Koncheyev, 'is for the Russian intelligentsia the image of Chernyshevski, which was spontaneously but accidentally carried away abroad by the émigrés, together with other, more useful things . . . Somebody suddenly confiscated the portrait.' "

At the end of *The Gift* Fyodor has grown the wings of a true poet, has drawn a luminous portrait of Russian literary art as he understands it, is happily and reciprocally in love with Zina, who is ready to go anywhere with him. Writing to his mother in Paris he remarks that while it is sheer sentimentality to expect to return to Russia, he can live more easily outside of his native country than some because he has taken away "the keys to her" — of language, art, and memory — and because some day "I shall live there in my books." *The Gift*, which is Nabokov's happiest book, is also his "goodbye to all that," the work in which he frees himself from his Russian past, narrowly and nostalgically considered, by earning a free entry into the vital dialogue of Russian art over the centuries. Both a summing up and a new starting point, it perhaps freed him also for the successful appropriation of a new language and culture when the European war drove him to American shores in 1940.

Like early Shakespearean comedy, for instance *Love's Labour's Lost, The Gift*, which is full of buried rhyming poetry and contains stanzas from *Eugene Onegin* written out as prose, takes delight in the processes of its own artifice. *Pale Fire*, on the other hand, is the work in which the devices cultivated lifelong by a great artist, the game he has been playing, the long dream of his imagination, are transmuted into something like the total dream and artifice of eternity. The 999-line poem in the novel, "neo-Popean" in technique and in its metaphysical arguments from design, and Wordsworthian in its autobiographical cast, is also Nabokov's "Sailing to Byzantium," while *Pale Fire* as a whole is a work like *The Tempest* in which the artist simply hands over his tools to the supreme artificer or artificers who control the ultimate dazzling game.

We can, I believe, brush aside the comic irony whereby John Francis Shade's fine poem is delivered into the hands of the bungling pedant and paranoid "editor," Kinbote, first because the poem, with its tail in its mouth, first line fused with last line, survives serene and intact, composing a magical, fiery circle which Kinbote, for all his incompetent "readings," unwarranted "emendations," and occasional outright forgings of "canceled lines," cannot violate; and second because, as Shade the poet knows, the work of imagination is unceasing, is owned by no one, and may even surface in the psychotic fantasy of a madman or in the egotistic inventions of an incompetent scholar. There are two great imaginative inventions tangled together in *Pale Fire*. One is Shade's autobiographical poem and the other is Kinbote's sad, funny, "true" autobiographical novel about the exiled King of Zembla, Charles the Beloved, which he composes through the devices of commentary and index. At a point in infinity, in the "involute abode" of uncreated fire and unfiltered light, at a point beyond entanglement and deception, the two "poems" are indeed identical, to each other and with all work of the imagination wrought at a sufficient intensity of longing for true, unimpeded vision.

That is of course from an ideal point of view. In "actuality," in the corporeal and phenomenal world, poems and other works of art are at best images and reminiscences of essence, working at the remove of reflected and diminished luminescence. Shade, with his subtle understanding of being as both utter mystery and perfect design, with all his unearthly poetic genius and his earthbound devotion to a beloved wife and a dead daughter, to strong drink and the rank comedy of faculty intrigue at Wordsmith U., comprehends fully that man's nature and human art can only fitfully reflect a perfection that lies elsewhere; which is why he qualifies the noun of his poem's title with the adjective "pale." And Kinbote, who professes religious orthodoxy and likes to argue the position against Shade's mystical agnosticism over the chessboard, reaches the same conclusion in different terms when he speaks of "God's Presence — a faint phosphorescence at first, a pale light in the dimness of bodily life, and a dazzling radiance after it."

One may see Shade's and Kinbote's relation as that of genius and its parasite or even that of Prospero to Caliban, but this ignores their mysterious rapport, the conspiratorial way that each of these lonely and eccentric figures serves and supports the other's deepest aspiration. Kinbote, who is in "fact" one V. Botkin, an American scholar of Russian descent recently discharged from a mental hospital, reinvents himself twice, as Charles Kinbote and as Charles the Beloved, thereby effecting a bizarre escape from "a personality consisting mainly of the shadows of its own prison bars." This illegal and mendacious procedure earns him the suspicious contempt of the dragonish faculty wife, Mrs. Hurley. But she is silenced when Shade speaks authoritatively and approvingly of "a person who deliberately peels off a drab and unhappy past and replaces it with a brilliant invention." As an artist he understands the sources, in human failure and heartbreak, of art's most brilliant contrivances and draws his friend in under the protection of that understanding. When Shade is dead and Kinbote first reads "Pale Fire" he is shocked to discover that the poem is not in fact the work called "Solus Rex," about the King of Zembla, which he had imagined Shade to be writing at his dictation. But then he rereads it: "I liked it better when expecting less. And what was that? What was that dim distant music, those vestiges of color in the air? Here and there

I discovered in it and especially, especially in the invaluable vari-
ants" (Kinbote's own forgeries) "echoes and spangles of my mind,
a long ripplewake of my glory." Even if the poem is not quite the
romaunt of Zembla the Fair, it will do almost as well, especially
now that he has the poem in his keeping: "My commentary to this
poem, now in the hands of my readers, represents an attempt to sort
out those echoes and wavelets of fire, and pale phosphorescent
hints, and all the many subliminal debts to me."

"*My* commentary . . . *my* readers . . . debts to *me*." Our pleas-
ure in this delicious satire on scholarly arrogance and bias is in-
tense but should not cause us to miss the point that Shade's *opus
posthumous*, from the standpoint of Shade's own playful artist's
temperament, has passed into the hands of its ideal editor, a fellow
artist. In short, there is a sense, only half absurd, in which Kinbote's
is a great scholarly commentary. For what other editor has ever
been present from the beginning, present throughout, and in at
the kill during the making of a great poem? The highest goal of
scholarship, which is to recapture the life out of which the masterpiece emerged, to capture the life of the poem as well, is served,
however lefthandedly, by Kinbote's scandalously unprofessional
commentary on "Pale Fire."

But Kinbote's most important service to John Shade is to con-
duct him to his death "from a bullet meant for another." It would
be tedious to demonstrate that Shade would not have died had he
never befriended Kinbote and, in particular, had he not gone stroll-
ing from his own house to Kinbote's to partake of the doubtful
pleasures of a dinner consisting of "a knackle of walnuts, a couple
of large tomatoes, and a bunch of bananas" washed down with Im-
perial Tokay wine. What is much more interesting is that Kinbote,
abetted no doubt by the "synchronizing phantom" of fate we have
noticed in other Nabokov works, delivers Shade to a death the
elderly poet is fully and hungrily prepared for.

The poem, "Pale Fire," is a tender recapitulation of Shade's attachments to and entanglements with the things of this world. It is full of affection for Sybil, the faithful wife, and agonized feeling for the ugly daughter whose suicide was the single tragic event of the couple's long, contented life together. And it takes delight in the sheer play of all phenomena as these reveal themselves to the poet's five senses or are recalled in their perfected "preterite" form through the artistry of memory. But the poet, from the very first couplet ("I was the shadow of the waxwing slain/ By the false azure in the windowpane"), casts his poem as a retrospection from the realm of death and joins himself with eager curiosity to the limitless mystery surrounding the little life his poem looks back upon. Each canto comes to center on a death experience — the momentary swoons ("a sudden sunburst in my head/ And then black night") he had known in childhood, the lonely dying of his daughter, his wonderfully cranky researches into death at the Institute of Preparation for the Hereafter — until the fourth canto, which is broken off before the second line of the concluding couplet of the whole poem falls into place.

It is broken off at the 999th line — "Trundling an empty barrow up the lane" — because Kinbote interrupts him with his importunate dinner suggestion. They walk across the yards to Kinbote's house. The assassin fires from the porch, Shade falls, and the poem completes itself: "I was the shadow of the waxwing slain." The poet vanishes into eternity by way of vanishing into his poem. We, and Kinbote, are left with a thousand lines (999 plus 1) making a perspective on a vanishing point of light and life receding into darkness. Perhaps this darkness, could one but view it along with Shade from the other side of life and death, would disclose itself as the very heart of light.

From a technical standpoint *Pale Fire* as novel triumphs over the most recalcitrant and inappropriate materials for fiction — a poem cum editorial notes and an index. Also, its striking subversion of the ordinary unitary conception of a fictional character — I am thinking of the schizoid editor's triple identity and the consequently shifting identities of such personages as Emerald-Izumrudov and Gradus, alias Jack Grey, alias d'Argus, etc., who pursue and harass him — makes good an old claim of Nabokov's that character to the artist in fiction is a "compositional resource" like any other, to be dissolved and reconstituted as freely and repeatedly as his themes require. But *Pale Fire* is something much more winning than a mere technical triumph. More than any other of his novels it shows a humane and tender sympathy for its imprisoned characters and seems to promise a final fulfillment of their immortal longings — if not now, sometime; if not here, then elsewhere.

⤴ Selected Bibliography

Works of Vladimir Nabokov

NOVELS AND COLLECTED SHORT STORIES

Mary (Mashen'ka). Berlin: "Slovo," 1926. English translation, New York: McGraw-Hill, 1970.

King, Queen, Knave (Korol', Dama, Valet). Berlin: "Slovo," 1928. English translation, New York: McGraw-Hill, 1968.

The Defense (Zashchita Luzhina). Berlin: "Slovo," 1930. English translation, New York: Putnam, 1964.

The Eye (Soglyadatay). Paris: Contemporary Annals, No. 44, 1930. English translation, New York: Phaedra, 1965.

Podvig [The Exploit]. Paris: Contemporary Annals, Nos. 45–48, 1932.

Camera Obscura (Kamera Obskura). Paris: Contemporary Annals, Nos. 49–52, 1932–33. English translation, London: John Long, 1936; American edition with author's alterations and retitled *Laughter in the Dark*, Indianapolis: Bobbs-Merrill, 1938.

Despair (Otchayanie). Berlin: Petropolis, 1936. English translation, New York: Putnam, 1966.

Invitation to a Beheading (Priglashenie na Kazn'). Paris: Dom Knigi, 1938. English translation, New York: Putnam, 1959.

The Gift (Dar). Paris: Contemporary Annals, Nos. 63–67, 1937–38 (without the fourth chapter). New York: Chekhov Publishing House, 1952 (complete). English translation, New York: Putnam, 1963.

The Real Life of Sebastian Knight. Norfolk, Conn.: New Directions, 1941.

Bend Sinister. New York: Henry Holt, 1947.

Lolita. Paris: Olympia Press, 1955.

Pnin. New York: Doubleday, 1957.

Nabokov's Dozen. New York: Doubleday, 1958. (Thirteen short stories.)

Pale Fire. New York: Putnam, 1962.

Nabokov's Quartet. New York: Phaedra, 1966. (Four long short stories.)

Ada, or Ardor: A Family Chronicle. New York: McGraw-Hill, 1969.

MEMOIRS

Conclusive Evidence. London: Victor Gollancz, 1951; New York: Harper, 1951.

46

Subsequently retitled in American reprintings *Speak, Memory*. Revised and expanded edition under latter title, New York: Putnam, 1966.
Drugiye Berega [Other Shores]. New York: Chekhov Publishing House, 1954.

VERSES

Poems. New York: Doubleday, 1959.

TRANSLATIONS

Three Russian Poets: Translations of Pushkin, Lermontov and Tiutchev. Norfolk, Conn.: New Directions, 1944.
The Song of Igor's Campaign. New York: Random House, 1960.
Eugene Onegin, by Aleksandr Pushkin. 4 vols. New York: Pantheon, 1964.

CRITICISM

Nikolai Gogol. Norfolk, Conn.: New Directions, 1944.

Bibliographies

Field, Andrew. "In Place of a Bibliography" and "Concluding Remarks," in *Nabokov: His Life in Art*. Boston: Little, Brown, 1967. Pp. 352–83.
Zimmer, Dieter E. *Vladimir Nabokov: Bibliographie des Gesamtwerks*. Hamburg: Rowohlt, 1963.

Critical and Biographical Studies

Appel, Alfred, ed. Vladimir Nabokov Issue, *Triquarterly*, 17 (Winter 1970).
Dembo, L. S., ed. *Nabokov the Man and His Works: Studies*. Madison: University of Wisconsin Press, 1967.
Dupee, F. W. "The Coming of Nabokov," in *"The King of the Cats" and Other Remarks on Writers and Writing*. New York: Farrar, Straus and Giroux, 1965. Pp. 117–41.
Field, Andrew. *Nabokov: His Life in Art*. Boston: Little, Brown, 1967.
Proffer, Karl. *Keys to Lolita*. Bloomington: Indiana University Press, 1968.
Smith, Peter Duval. "Vladimir Nabokov on His Life and Work," *Listener*, 68:856–58 (November 22, 1962). (Text of broadcast interview.)
Stegner, Page. *Escape into Aesthetics: The Art of Vladimir Nabokov*. New York: Dial, 1966.